THANKSGIVING

BY ANN HEINRICHS • ILLUSTRATED BY CHARLES JORDAN

Published in the United States of America by The Child's World®
PO Box 326 • Chanhassen, MN 55317-0326
800-599-READ • www.childsworld.com

ACKNOWLEDGMENTS

The Child's World®: Mary Berendes, Publishing Director

Editorial Directions, Inc.: E. Russell Primm, Editorial Director; Katie Marsico, Managing Editor; Judith Shiffer, Assistant Editor; Caroline Wood and Rory Mabin, Editorial Assistants; Susan Hindman, Copy Editor and Proofreader; Elizabeth Nellums, Rory Mabin, Ruth Martin, and Caroline Wood, Fact Checkers; Tim Griffin/IndexServ, Indexer

The Design Lab: Kathleen Petelinsek, Design and Page Production

LIBRARY OF CONGRESS CATALOGING-IN-PUBLICATION DATA

Heinrichs, Ann.
  Thanksgiving / by Ann Heinrichs; illustrated by Charles Jordan.
    p. cm. — (Holidays, festivals, & celebrations)
  Includes index.
  ISBN 1-59296-582-2 (library bound : alk. paper)
  1. Thanksgiving Day—Juvenile literature. 2. United States—Social life and customs—Juvenile literature. I. Jordan, Charles, ill. II. Title. III. Series.
  GT4975.T45 2006
  394.2649—dc22   2005025689

TABLE OF CONTENTS

CHAPTER ONE

HAPPY THANKSGIVING!

Big, fat cardboard turkeys decorate the walls. Delicious smells drift from the kitchen. And here comes the pumpkin pie. It's Thanksgiving!

Thanksgiving is a warm and friendly time. Family members gather together. Often they travel from far away. Friends are welcome, too. They enjoy a delicious feast together.

Above all, they give thanks. They give thanks for a rich **harvest** that brings them plenty of food. They give thanks for all they have. And they give thanks for each other. What a happy holiday!

Thanksgiving is a time to enjoy delicious foods and celebrate family and friends.

CHAPTER TWO

CELEBRATING THE HARVEST

Many **ancient** people had harvest festivals. They gave thanks for their plentiful farm products. Ancient Greeks and Romans had goddesses of farm products. To the Greeks, the goddess was Demeter. For the Romans, she was Ceres. Both peoples made offerings to their goddess in the fall. They offered corn, fruit, and pigs.

In ancient Egypt, spring was harvest time. Then Egyptians held a festival in honor of Min. He was the god of the harvest. A big parade was held. There were dancing, sports events, and offerings.

Ancient people had special gods and goddesses for crops.

The word cereal comes from the name of the goddess Ceres.

THANKSGIVING COMES AGAIN

The year has turned its circle,
The seasons come and go.
The harvest all is gathered in
And chilly north winds blow.

Orchards have shared their
*   treasures,*
The fields, their yellow grain,
So open wide the doorway—
Thanksgiving comes again!
—Author unknown

CHAPTER THREE

LIFE IN A NEW LAND

America's Thanksgiving began with the Pilgrims. The Pilgrims were a religious group. They originally lived in England. But their beliefs were not welcome there. So they left to find a new home.

The Pilgrims sailed to the New World. This land would become the United States. The Pilgrims set sail in 1620. Their ship was called the *Mayflower*. The Pilgrims settled in Plymouth. They built the Plymouth **Colony.** That site is now in Massachusetts.

Life was hard in their new land. Winters were bitterly cold. But Native Americans helped the Pilgrims out. They gave the newcomers seeds. They showed them how to grow corn.

Native Americans helped the Pilgrims survive in their new land.

THE PILGRIMS CAME

The Pilgrims came
across the sea,
And never thought
of you and me;
And yet it's very strange
the way
We think of them
Thanksgiving Day.

We tell their story,
old and true
Of how they sailed
across the blue,
And found a new land
to be free
And built their homes
quite near the sea.

Every child knows well the tale
Of how they bravely
    turned the sail
And journeyed many
    a day and night,
To worship God as they
    thought right.

The people think that
    they were sad
And grave; I'm sure that
    they were glad—
They made Thanksgiving
    Day—that's fun!
We thank the Pilgrims,
    every one!
—Annette Wynne

CHAPTER FOUR

A GREAT FEAST

I n the fall, the Pilgrims had a rich harvest. They were thankful. They wanted to share with their Native American friends. The Pilgrims invited them to a big meal.

Canada has a Thanksgiving Day, too. It's the second Monday in October.

Thanks to the Native Americans, the Pilgrims had a plentiful harvest.

THE FIRST
THANKSGIVING DAY

*Heap high the board with
plenteous cheer, and
gather to the feast,
And toast that sturdy
Pilgrim band whose courage
never ceased.
Give praise to that All-
Gracious One by whom
their steps were led,
And thanks unto the
harvest's Lord who
sends our daily bread.
—Alice Williams Brotherton
(1848–1930)*

Chief Massasoit came with ninety Indians. They
brought five deer to eat. The Pilgrims provided
ducks, geese, and turkeys. They served fish and
corn, too. The feast was held outdoors. It went on
for three days! We look back on this as the first
Thanksgiving.

*The Pilgrims and the Indians shared
the first Thanksgiving feast for three days.*

CHAPTER FIVE

BECOMING A HOLIDAY

The Pilgrims' feast only happened once. It did not immediately become a holiday. But thanksgiving days were common in the colonies. They were days of prayer. People gave thanks for their many blessings.

In time, the colonies became the United States. Some states held days of thanksgiving. But many people wanted a holiday for the whole country.

President Abraham Lincoln agreed. In 1863, he declared a national day of thanksgiving. Now we all celebrate Thanksgiving Day. When is it? The fourth Thursday in November!

A big Thanksgiving dinner reminds us of how lucky we are to have plentiful food to eat.

THOUGHTS OF THANKSGIVING

Thanksgiving day is coming soon,
That long remembered day
When nature gives her blessed boon
To all America....

The roast goose, steaming
*   on the plate,*
The sweet potato cobbler,
The cranberry sauce,
*   the pudding baked,*
The seasoned turkey gobbler,

All these delights and many more,
From north, south, west and east,
Do all the nation keep in store
For this Thanksgiving feast....
—Charles Frederick White
*   (1876–?)*

CHAPTER SIX

THANKSGIVING DINNER

Thanksgiving dinner is delicious! We eat many **traditional** foods then. The main dish is turkey. It's stuffed with dressing. Some people call it stuffing.

Many side dishes round out the meal. One is cranberry sauce. Another is sweet potatoes. Mashed potatoes and gravy are served, too.

Some families have their own special customs. They may serve goose or duck instead of turkey. Italian Americans serve pasta. And people who live near the ocean might serve crab.

What's for dessert? Pumpkin pie! Other favorites are pecan and mincemeat pie. Mincemeat is a chopped mixture of raisins, apples, and spices.

No Thanksgiving meal would be complete without a slice of delicious pie!

THANKSGIVING TIME

When all the leaves are
  off the boughs,
And nuts and apples gathered in,
And cornstalks waiting
  for the cows,
And pumpkins safe
  in barn and bin,
Then Mother says,
  "My children dear,
The fields are brown,
  and autumn flies;
Thanksgiving Day is very near,
And we must make
  thanksgiving pies!"
—Author unknown

CHAPTER SEVEN

DECORATIONS AND SYMBOLS

There are many Thanksgiving decorations. Like turkeys! They can be made of paper or cardboard. They are big and fat. And their tail feathers spread out like a fan.

Pilgrim hats are another decoration. The Pilgrims wore mostly black clothes. Men wore black hats with wide brims. On the front was a shiny buckle.

Some people decorate with fall crops. They use corn, pumpkins, and squash. Indian corn is a favorite. It has grains of many colors.

The cornucopia (cor-nuh-KOH-pee-uh) is

a Thanksgiving **symbol**. It's called the horn of plenty. The cornucopia is a food basket. It's curved like an animal's horn. It overflows with fruits and vegetables. It reminds us of our blessings. We live in a land of plenty. We have much to be thankful for!

The cornucopia reminds us of all that we have to be thankful for.

AT GRANDMA'S HOUSE

I like the taste of turkey
Any time throughout the year
But it never seems to taste as
*   good*
As when Thanksgiving's here.

Could be it's all the trimmings
That are cooked with it to eat—
But I think it's eating at
*   Grandma's house*
That makes it such a treat!
—Author unknown

CHAPTER EIGHT

THE POETS' CORNER

The New-England Boy's Song about Thanksgiving Day

*Over the river, and
 through the wood,
To grandfather's house we go;
The horse knows the way,
To carry the sleigh,
Through the white and
 drifted snow.*

*Over the river, and
 through the wood,
To grandfather's house away!
We would not stop
For doll or top,
For 'tis Thanksgiving Day.*

Over the river, and
    through the wood,
Oh, how the wind
    does blow!
It stings the toes,
And bites the nose,
As over the ground we go.

Over the river, and
    through the wood,
With a clear blue
    winter sky,
The dogs do bark,
And children hark,
As we go jingling by.

Over the river, and
    through the wood,
To have a first-rate play—
Hear the bells ring
Ting a ling ding,
Hurra for Thanksgiving
    Day!

Over the river, and
    through the wood—
No matter for winds
    that blow;
Or if we get
The sleigh upset,
Into a bank of snow.

Over the river, and
   through the wood,
To see little John and Ann;
We will kiss them all,
And play snow-ball,
And stay as long as we can.

Over the river, and
   through the wood,
Trot fast, my dapple grey!
Spring over the ground,
Like a hunting hound,
For 'tis Thanksgiving Day!

Over the river, and
 through the wood,
And straight through the
 barn-yard gate;
We seem to go
Extremely slow,
It is so hard to wait.

Over the river, and
 through the wood—
Old Jowler hears our bells;
He shakes his **pow**,
With a loud bow wow,
And thus the news he tells.

Over the river, and
 through the wood—
When grandmother
 sees us come,
She will say, Oh dear,
The children are here,
Bring a pie for every one.

Over the river, and
 through the wood—
Now grandmother's
 cap I spy!
Hurra for the fun!
Is the pudding done?
Hurra for the pumpkin pie!

—Lydia Maria Child
(1802–1880)

Joining in the Spirit of Thanksgiving

- What does your family do on Thanksgiving Day? Write a short story telling about it.

- Draw a Thanksgiving tree. It will begin as a tree with several branches. Draw the leaves one by one. On each leaf, write the name of something you are thankful for.

- Does your community have a shelter or kitchen for homeless people? Ask if you can help out on Thanksgiving Day.

- Some organizations deliver meals to people on Thanksgiving. Does this happen in your community? See if you can join in.

- Do you know someone from another country? Ask how his or her country celebrates a day of thanksgiving.

- Try out a new idea: Every day is a time to give thanks for all we have!

Making Thanksgiving Cornbread

Ingredients:
1 cup cornmeal
1 cup all-purpose flour
¼ cup sugar
1 tablespoon baking powder
1 teaspoon salt
1 cup milk
⅓ cup vegetable oil
1 egg
Cooking spray

Directions:
Preheat the oven to 400 degrees Fahrenheit.* Mix the cornmeal, flour, sugar, baking powder, and salt in a medium-sized bowl. In a smaller bowl, stir the milk, vegetable oil, and egg. Next, pour the milk mixture into the medium bowl. Be sure to stir until all the ingredients are completely blended. Use cooking spray to lightly coat the bottom of a loaf pan. Pour the mixture into the pan and bake twenty to twenty-five minutes. Allow the cornbread to cool for about thirty minutes before removing it from the pan. Pass your treat around the Thanksgiving table—it should serve about eight people!

Have an adult help you operate the oven.

Making Personalized Thanksgiving Napkins

Dress up your Thanksgiving table and let your family members know why you are thankful for them with this fun project.

What you need:

One plain white cloth napkin for each family member
Permanent markers or fabric pens

Instructions:

1. Open a napkin and lay it flat on a table
2. Write the name of a family member on the napkin
3. Write a few words that tell why you are thankful to have that person as part of your family
4. Repeat steps 1 through 3 until you have a napkin for each person in your family
5. Place each person's napkin beside their dinner plate.

Variation: If you don't have cloth napkins to work with, you can make paper placemats to use on your Thanksgiving table. Just substitute a large piece of white paper for the napkin in step 1.

That's it! If you'd like, you can invite other members of your family to add their thanks to each napkin. You can also draw pictures of turkeys or other Thanksgiving symbols on them.

Words to Know

ancient *(AYN-shunt)* very old; often meaning thousands of years old

boon *(BOON)* a gift

colony *(KOLL-uh-nee)* a new land with ties to another country

harvest *(HAR-vuhst)* crops that are gathered in

pow *(POW)* old word for "head"

symbol *(SIM-buhl)* an object that stands for an idea

traditional *(truh-DISH-uh-null)* following long-held customs

How to Learn More about Thanksgiving

At the Library

Bruchac, Joseph, and Greg Shed. *Squanto's Journey: The Story of the First Thanksgiving.* San Diego: Silver Whistle, 2000.

Erlbach, Arlene, and Herbert Erlbach. *Thanksgiving Day Crafts.* Berkeley Heights, N.J.: Enslow Publishers, 2005.

Grace, Catherine O'Neill, Margaret M. Bruchac, Sisse Brimberg (photographer), and Cotton Coulson (photographer). *1621: A New Look at Thanksgiving.* Washington, D.C.: National Geographic Society, 2001.

Osborne, Mary Pope, and Sal Murdocca (illustrator). *Thanksgiving on Thursday.* New York: Random House, 2002.

On the Web

Visit our home page for lots of links about Thanksgiving:
http://www.childsworld.com/links

NOTE TO PARENTS, TEACHERS, AND LIBRARIANS:
We routinely verify our Web links to make sure they're safe,
active sites—so encourage your readers to check them out!

ABOUT THE AUTHOR

Ann Heinrichs lives in Chicago, Illinois. She has written more than two hundred books for children. She loves traveling to faraway places.

ABOUT THE ILLUSTRATOR

Charles Jordan is a freelance illustrator whose illustrations appear in many magazines, books, and other publications for children. He lives in Pennsylvania.

Index